Oregon Air Guard F-4C Phantom
takes on gas below a KC-135 tanker.

TOP GUN
FIGHTERS
& AMERICA'S JET POWER

BEEKMAN HOUSE

A handsome diamond of F-4C Phantom fighter-bombers operated by the Oregon Air National Guard.

CONTENTS

TAKEOFF	4
FIGHTER JETS	6
F-4	8
F-5E	20
F-14	26
F-15	40
F-16	54
F/A-18	66
F-106	80
F-111	84
ATTACK JETS	94
A-4	96
A-6E	104
A-7	114
A-10	124
AV-8B	132

RECONNAISSANCE PLANES	138
SR-71	140
RF-4	146
TR-1	156
U-2	158
TRAINER JETS	160
T-38	162
T-2	166
T-33	168
ELECTRONIC JETS	170
EA-6B	172
E-3	178
E-2C	180
GLOSSARY	186

h g f e d c b

This edition published by Beekman House, Distributed by Crown Publishers, Inc., 225 Park Avenue South, New York, New York 10003

ISBN 0-517-65580-2

Library of Congress Card Number: 87-63424

Text and Photos by George Hall

Front Cover: A-4 Skyhawk

Back Cover: F-4 Phantom

TAKEOFF

America's defensive power takes many forms—troops and armor on land, huge fleets on and beneath the oceans, a strategic deterrent of intercontinental missiles to guard against global nuclear war. But to most interested observers, nothing can be more exciting and awe-inspiring than the aerial maneuvers of our screaming, gleaming military jets.

Airplanes first went into battle in World War I, almost 75 years ago. The planes of that day were underpowered, piston-engined, propeller-driven crates made of wood, wire, and cloth. But even the most inflexible old-timers in the military establishment could see that warfare would be utterly changed by the presence of the planes. Troops, and even colossal battleships, could be successfully attacked from high above. Military movements could be easily witnessed and photographed from a bird's-eye vantage point. By World War II, two decades later, major tide-turning struggles such as the Battle of Britain and the epic naval clash near Midway Island were being fought entirely by airplanes flying hundreds of miles to meet in aerial dogfights.

Jet propulsion made its entrance late in the second world war in the form of an astonishing German fighter-bomber, the Me 262, that could outfly anything in the skies. Today, practically every one of the more than two hundred American military aircraft types is jet powered—either by pure turbojets and turbofans or by turbines that turn conventional propellers.

The jet engine has proven to be one of the greatest advances in aviation history; modern jet powerplants can turn out as much as twenty times the horsepower per pound of engine weight as the old-fashioned reciprocating gasoline motors of a generation ago. Jet engines also have far fewer moving parts. Jets work by pulling in air through an intake, and greatly compressing it in a set of fast-spinning turbine blades. The compressed air is mixed with kerosinelike fuel and burned. As the hot exhaust blasts from the exhaust tube, the aircraft is pushed forward with a tremendous force called *thrust.*

Even greater thrust can be generated when jet engines are fitted with *afterburners.* These devices squirt raw fuel into the hot exhaust, with the resulting explosion almost doubling the engine's power output. Any jet seen with a trail that resembles a rocketlike plume of fire is in "full burner." The hottest jet fighters can crank out the equivalent of over 40,000 horsepower with the afterburners lit.

America's air power is organized into several different air forces, each with its own set of missions, training objectives, and hardware. The U.S. Air Force is by far the largest in total personnel and equipment. The Air Force operates tactical forces in Europe and the Far East, as well as strategic bomber wings and the huge Military Airlift Command (its own transport airline). Air Force planes are also flown by state-controlled Air National Guard squadrons all over the United States.

Top Gun students in their F-14 Tomcats form up with two instructors in A-4 Mangoose single-seaters (left).

Naval aviation is geared to maritime security, protection of surface and undersea fleets, and the support of special military missions abroad. Many, although not all, naval pilots are skilled in perhaps the most difficult routine feat in all flying—operating a red-hot jet from the pitching steel deck of an aircraft carrier in any kind of weather.

The Navy's very best carrier fighter pilots are invited to attend the Navy Fighter Weapons School, *Top Gun*, a five-week "graduate school" in fighter and dogfighting tactics given at Miramar Naval Air Station in San Diego. Top Gun grew out of the rather poor showing by American fighter pilots in the early years of the Vietnam War; in switching to ultramodern jet fighters with air-to-air missiles

instead of the guns of old, many valuable dogfighting lessons had been forgotten and had to be relearned. A Top Gun graduate today is as capable as any fighter pilot on earth.

The U.S. Marine Corps is a semi-independent military assault force equipped with its own ships, tanks, and a small but very complete air force with everything from jet fighters to transports and helicopters.

The Army also has a large "air force," made up almost totally of thousands of helicopters plus a smattering of fixed-wing planes. The Army has no jets.

The Army and Air Force each operate their own independent training systems to crank out hundreds of new pilots every year. Since naval flying is so different, it too operates a separate

pilot-training structure at bases near the Gulf of Mexico. Marine Corps and U.S. Coast Guard pilots train alongside their Navy colleagues before splitting off into their own specialties.

We're going to take a closer look at the most awesome fighting jets in America's arsenal, each with a mission specialty that it can accomplish better than any other bird in the world. We'll fly with the fighters, the ground-attack jets, the photo-reconnaissance birds that gauge the enemy's intentions, the electronics-laden control and jamming planes, and the trainers that give the budding jet jockeys their first addictive taste in the very fastest of fast lanes. You will, as Maverick Mitchell says in the movie *Top Gun*, "Feel the need for speed!"

5

FIGHTER JETS

Since their introduction to warfare over the trenches of World War I, fighter aircraft have been looked upon as knights of the skies, locked in lonely, furious combat with their opposite numbers. Fighters mainly ignore the larger ground or sea battle; their role is to engage and destroy the aircraft of the enemy in midair. Modern American fighters are without question the most powerful and capable in the world; most of the countries of the free world use American-made fighter jets for their own air defense.

American fighter duties are handled principally by an awesome quartet of jets known, because of their designation num-

Two Louisiana Air Guard F-15 Eagles roll away from the setting sun south of New Orleans.

bers, as the "teen fighters." The Navy and Marine Corps, operating from aircraft carriers and land bases, fly the F-14 Tomcat (of the movie *Top Gun* fame) and the spectacular new F/A-18 Hornet, a dual-role fighter that can effortlessly double as a ground-attack bomber. The Air Force and Air National Guard fly the F-15 Eagle interceptor and the red-hot little F-16 Fighting Falcon,

hundreds of which have also been put into service by the NATO countries and other allies.

Besides these existing fighters, we'll take a fond look back at the F-4 Phantom, the premier jet of the Vietnam era and still a major contender in the 1980's. Also reviewed in this section are the F-5E Tiger II, a hot but simple little fighter designed for the export market; the beautiful delta-

winged F-106; and the immense F-111 Aardvark, which is really a long-range penetration bomber with an "F" designation.

So let's zip up our G-suits, check our six o'clock (that's straight astern in fighter talk, where the bogey usually hides), and see what jet-powered dog-fighting is all about.

F-4 PHANTOM II

A Marine Reserve F-4 Phantom with its canopy up at Marine Corps Station Kaneohe, Hawaii.

"Double Ugly"

The F-4 Phantom fighter-bomber electrified military aviation when it came upon the scene in the early sixties. When new, the F-4 represented a quantum leap in fighter-interceptor design—performance vastly superior to anything that went before, and a battery of radar-guided and heat-seeking missiles for air combat. It evolved into a ground-attack bomber, which was not its original mission. It was the Navy's first serious long-range fleet-defense interceptor and a major player in Vietnam for the Navy, Marines, and Air Force.

The Phantom, nicknamed "Double Ugly" or "Rhino," is in the twilight of its service with the American air forces. It remains on duty with the active Air Force as an air defense fighter, attack bomber, and all-weather photo-reconnaissance aircraft. It's still the plane of choice for the harsh and dangerous "Wild Weasel" mission—teasing and then attacking enemy ground-to-air missile batteries. The Weasels streak into the target area ahead of the attacking strike package, daring the ground defenders to lock them up with their search radars. If the bad guys take the bait, they'll be the recipients of devastating antiradiation missiles that literally fly down the radar beam to its source.

The Phantom is still big, fast, noisy, and tremendously exciting to watch in action. But it has trouble "turning and burning" with the newer teen jets in a one-vs.-one fight, and these older jets are cranky and hard to maintain in their old age. We'll see the Phantom in service for at least another decade, though, as Weasels, reconnaissance planes, and Reserve/National Guard fighters. A huge following of Phantom lovers will hate to see it go.

Marine Corps Reserve Phantoms,
photographed from a camera pod on
a third jet, streak at a low altitude
over the coast of Molokai, Hawaii.

A pair of tightly welded Marine Corps Phantoms about to begin a low-level attack exercise over the Arizona desert.

11

An Air National Guard Phantom in a right turn from Hickam AFB, Hawaii.

12

Earlier Phantoms were burdened with smoky engines that made them painfully easy to spot in a dogfight. Most have now been refitted with smokeless powerplants.

A ground crew loads 500-pound bombs onto a Marine Phantom.

A Marine F-4 uses full afterburner to blast into the Arizona sunset.

Two Phantom crew members—pilot up front, weapons systems officer in the back seat—mount up for a pre-dawn hop at Nellis AFB, Nevada.

Two F-4 Phantoms of the Oregon National Guard move in "welded wing" formation.

16

An F-4 Phantom pilot yanks the big bird into a steep bank.

Marine Phantoms drop down to use terrain as a shield prior to starting their bomb runs.

18

SPECIFICATIONS

F-4 PHANTOM II

Manufacturer: McDonnell Aircraft Company

Military branch: Air Force, Air National Guard, Marine Corps, Navy

Type: Carrier- and land-based fighter; reconnaissance capability

Engines: Twin General Electric afterburning turbojets

Maximum speed: 1,500 mph (Mach 2.27)

Wingspan: 38 ft. 5 in.

Length: 58 ft. 3 in. to 63 ft.

Height: 16 ft. 3 in.

Weight: [Empty] 28,000 to 30,900 lbs.; [maximum loaded] 54,600 lb. to 60,360 lb.

Weapons systems: Four AIM-7 Sparrow missiles; 20-millimeter M61 gun; five weapons stations for maximum load of 16,000 lbs.

Crew: Pilot; radar operator

First flight: 1958

Service entry: 1960

19

F-5E
TIGER II

The small, simple F-5E Tiger II was designed to be exported to foreign air forces around the world. American Air Force and Navy pilots fly them as adversary fighters, simulating enemy tactics in practice dogfights.

"Little Giant"

The beautiful little F-5E Tiger II, with its slippery pop-bottle fuselage, needle nose, and razor-thin wings, looks awfully modern for a jet that has been around for about twenty years. Modeled after the F-5A Freedom Fighter, the F-5E was initially designed specifically as a simple-to-fly, simple-to-maintain fighter for export sale to countries that needed a fighter capability but couldn't afford to buy and operate the latest thing. There was to be no niche for the plane in the U.S. military inventory.

Nevertheless, the Pentagon did buy a bunch in the 1970's for one special mission—the simulation of enemy supersonic fighters (particularly the Soviet MiG-21, which it closely resembles) in training dogfights with top Navy, Marine, and Air Force fighter jocks. The Air Force currently operates four squadrons of Tigers as "Aggressors," done up in an array of Russian and Third-World camouflage paint jobs and sporting those over-sized nose numbers the Soviets like so much. The Navy's Top Gun school also uses the F-5E in the same way, although its Tiger collection, exhausted after fifteen years of daily yank-and-bank dogfighting with the best Tomcat and Hornet pilots, is now being replaced by brand-new F-16 adversaries.

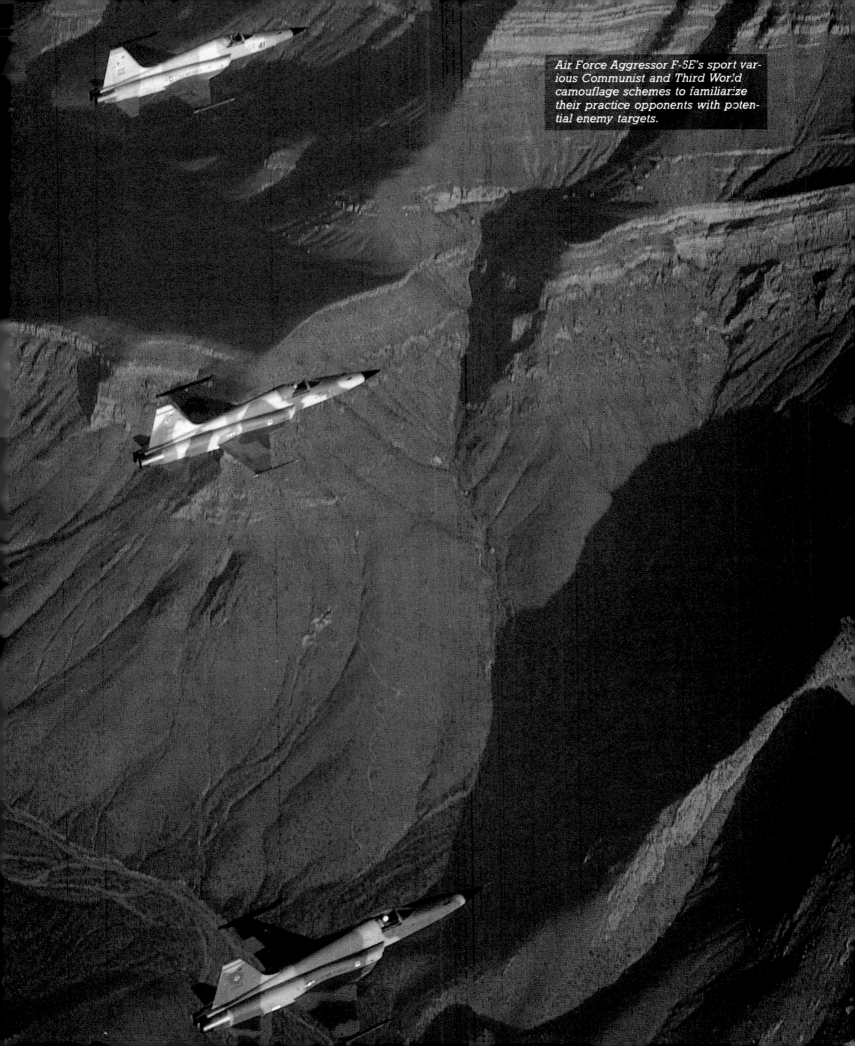

Air Force Aggressor F-5E's sport various Communist and Third World camouflage schemes to familiarize their practice opponents with potential enemy targets.

An Aggressor pilot mounts a Tiger at RAF Alconbury, England. Large nose numbers are a fixture on all Russian fighters.

A perfect formation of F-5E Tiger IIs, operated by the 65th Aggressor Squadron, Nellis AFB, Nevada. The planes are painted in camouflage schemes common to countries of the Warsaw Pact.

23

SPECIFICATIONS

F-5E TIGER II

Manufacturer: Northrop Corporation

Military branch: Air Force, Navy

Type: Tactical fighter

Engines: Twin General Electric J85-21 afterburning turbojets

Maximum speed: 1,077 mph (Mach 1.63)

Wingspan: 26 ft. 8 in.

Length: 47 ft. 2 in.

Height: 13 ft. 2 in.

Weight: [Empty] 9,683 lb.; [maximum loaded] 24,676 lb.

Weapons systems: Two 20-millimeter M-39A2 guns; two AIM-9 missiles; ordnance totaling 7,000 lb.

Crew: Pilot

First flight: 1969

Service entry: 1973

An Air Force Aggressor lets fly with the traditional Gomer go-sign before a dogfight over the Nevada desert.

25

F-14
TOMCAT

The F-14 Tomcat is huge for a fighter—but amazingly agile in a dogfight.

"Top Gun"

The world's premier air-defense interceptor is the immense F-14 Tomcat, the undisputed aerial star of the movie *Top Gun* and dreaded foe of any adversary intending to attack an American surface fleet. The carrier-based Tomcat is a twin-engine fighter with variable-sweep wings (wing sweep that can be varied in flight, or folded for easier storage aboard a carrier). It has a two-member crew—pilot up front, Radar Intercept Officer (RIO) handling radar and weapons in the back.

The fighting extension of the Tomcat is its six AIM-54 Phoenix air-to-air missiles, coupled with superradar that can track 24 different aerial targets simultaneously and launch the Phoenix missiles (or shorter-range Sparrow and Sidewinder missiles) at the most threatening adversary. The big jet also packs a six-barrel 20-millimeter Gatling-type gun for close-range attacks, in case any bogies somehow slip past the missile screen.

The Tomcat is huge for a fighter. The general feeling in the fighter world is that smaller is better—the smaller you are, the harder you are to see. And the Tomcat can be seen forever. But, despite its large size, it is an incredibly agile dogfighter, able to slow down and turn like crazy when the pilot motors those gigantic, variable swing wings into the forward position. All current and new Tomcats will soon be getting the far superior General Electric F-110 turbofan engines, giving them the energy they've needed for world-class air combat maneuvering (ACM).

An F-14 with its wings in the farthest aft position for carrier storage.

"Maverick" and "Iceman" form up over a Fallon, Nevada, dry lake bed during the filming of Top Gun.

28

Top Gun students get ready to take their big Tomcat down into the weeds at Fallon, Nevada, in an effort to elude "enemy" instructors.

An F-14 pilot's view of the landing lineup prior to trapping on the USS Constellation. *Steel arresting cables 1½ inches thick will drag the thirty-ton jet to a complete stop in a little over a hundred yards.*

A Tomcat about to enter the landing pattern over the USS Constellation.

203

Tomcats line up for heart-stopping "cat shots" (catapult takeoffs) aboard the USS Enterprise.

A Tomcat catches a good 3-wire, the ideal choice among the carrier's four arresting cables.

Tomcats retract their variable-geometry wings into the full-sweep position for storage on the usually crowded carrier deck.

33

Carrier deck director carefully moves a Tomcat of a Naval Reserve squadron into the catapult of the USS Ranger.

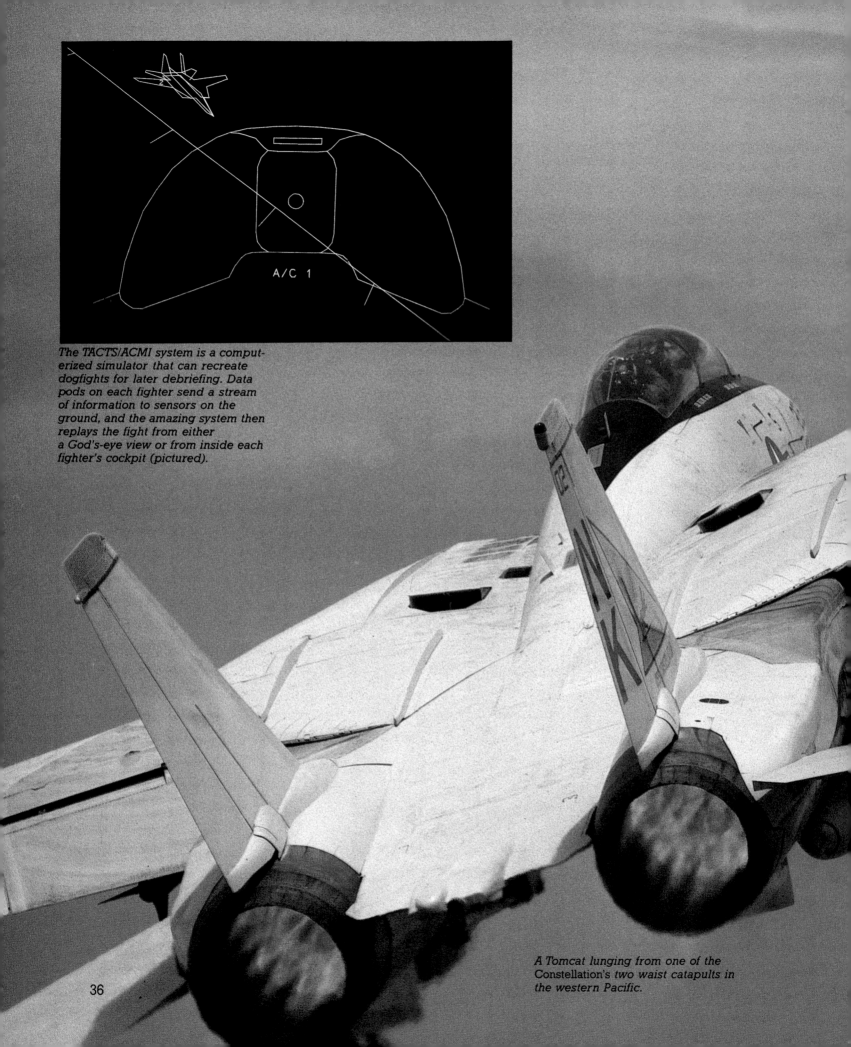

The TACTS/ACMI system is a computerized simulator that can recreate dogfights for later debriefing. Data pods on each fighter send a stream of information to sensors on the ground, and the amazing system then replays the fight from either a God's-eye view or from inside each fighter's cockpit (pictured).

A/C 1

A Tomcat lunging from one of the Constellation's two waist catapults in the western Pacific.

F-14 RIO (Radar Intercept Officer) grabs a self-portrait as the wingman slides into a trail position.

Crew members load a Tomcat with a deadly load of Sparrow missiles prior to a practice shoot against an unmanned target drone. The Sparrow is guided to its victim by the powerful radar of its mother plane.

An F-14 Tomcat in a sunset catapult launch from the carrier USS Constellation.

F-14 TOMCAT

Manufacturer: Grumman Aerospace Corporation

Military branch: Navy

Type: Carrier-based multi-role fighter

Engines: Twin Pratt & Whitney TF30-412A or 414A afterburning turbofans; General Electric F110-400 afterburning turbofans

Maximum speed: 1,544 mph (Mach 2.34)

Wingspan: [68-degree sweep] 38 ft. 2 in.; [20-degree sweep] 64 ft. 1½ in.

Length: 62 ft. 8 in.

Height: 16 ft. 0 in.

Weight: [Empty] 40,104 lb.; [maximum loaded] 74,348 lb.

Weapons systems: One 20-millimeter M61-A1 gun; four AIM-7 Sparrow missiles and four or eight AIM-9 Sidewinder missiles, or six AIM-54 Phoenix missiles and two AIM-9 Sidewinder missiles; maximum weapon load of 14,500 lb.

Crew: Pilot; observer

First flight: 1970

Service entry: 1972

F-15
EAGLE

F-15s from Bitburg, Germany fly a "Zulu Alert" mission to check out possible intruders from the other side of the Iron Curtain. The alert is maintained with four fully armed jets, 24 hours a day. The Eagles can be hurtling down the runway within three minutes of getting an alarm.

"Foxbat Killer"

The F-15 Eagle is a big, bad, air defense fighter, designed for use by overland air forces. Although its size and twin vertical tails make it look much like the Tomcat, the F-15 is a completely different plane, with fixed geometry (nonmovable) wings and a single pilot on board.

In its air-defense mode, it can carry four Sparrow radar missiles, four Sidewinder heat-seeking missiles for the close-in fight, and the same 20-millimeter cannon carried in the Tomcat. In its prime, nothing in the skies rivaled the F-15 in close-in combat; not even the Soviet's ultra-fast "Foxbat," the MiG 25 spy plane. (In fact, the F-15 became known as the "Foxbat Killer.")

The F-15 has seen plenty of combat in the Middle East, and it has earned quite a reputation for blowing the enemy planes right out of the skies. Designed to be "user-friendly," the F-15 earns the highest praise from the jockeys who drive them.

Newly introduced is the F-15E Strike Eagle, a two-seater with uprated engines being readied for the deep ground-strike missions now being handled by the F-111.

A duet of F-15 Eagles flown by Louisiana Air National Guard. This highly experienced New Orleans fighter outfit was first in the Guard to receive this ultramodern Eagle.

41

A two-ship of F-15 Eagles out of Bit-burg, Germany pull into an effortless turn high over Ardennes, Belgium.

An Eagle drops a target "dart" for aerial gunnery practice. Dart will be reeled out on a cable a half mile behind the jet to guard against accidental hits. A microphone in the dart will record near misses as 20-millimeter bullets flash past.

Realistic cockpit simulator allows Eagle pilots to practice many procedures without actually flying expensive jets.

"Zulu Alert" Eagles at Bitburg, Germany are loaded with live Sparrow and Sidewinder air-to-air missiles, four of each per jet. The Eagle also carries a 20-millimeter multibarrel cannon for close-in fights.

Crew chief communicates over intercom with F-15 pilot during engine start-up.

An elegant four-ship formation of Eagles flies high over Holloman AFB, New Mexico.

Bitburg Eagles twist and turn in a friendly mock dogfight over the Belgium practice area.

47

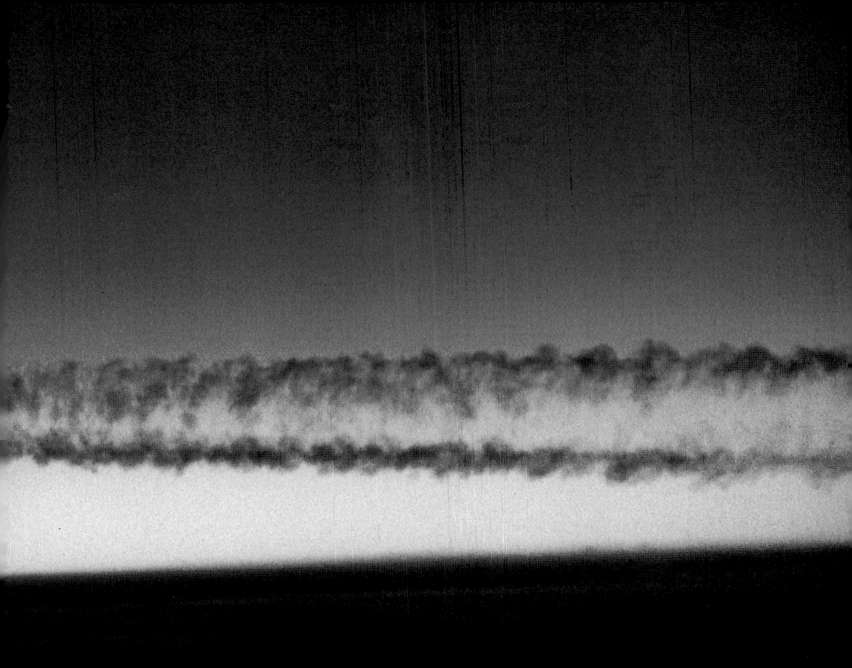

An F-15 streaks ahead of its high altitude contrail as the sun sets over the Gulf of Mexico.

Exhaust burners and afterburners in the F-15 Eagles. Pratt & Whitney F 100-100 engines can blast out more than 47,000 pounds of thrust in full burner.

An Eagle of the Louisiana National Guard spits flame from its afterburners as it takes off at NAS New Orleans.

51

Two F-15 Eagle fighters based at Bitburg. West Germany.

SPECIFICATIONS

F-15 EAGLE

Manufacturer: McDonnell Douglas Aircraft Company

Military branch: Air Force, Air National Guard

Type: Fighter; attack capability

Engines: Twin Pratt & Whitney F100-100 afterburning turbofans

Maximum speed: 1,650 mph (Mach 2.50)

Wingspan: 42 ft. 9¾ in.

Length: 63 ft. 9 in.

Height: 18 ft. 5½ in.

Weight: [Empty] 27,381 lb.; [maximum loaded] 56,000 lb.

Weapons systems: One 20-millimeter M61A1 gun; four AIM-7 Sparrow missiles or eight AIM-120A plus four AIM-9 Sidewinder missiles; external load of 16,000 lb.

Crew: Pilot

First flight: 1972

Service entry: 1974

F-16
FIGHTING FALCON

Brand new F-16s on a transatlantic delivery flight to Hahn, Germany. Jets will refuel six times during the eight-hour crossing.

"Electric Jet"

The General Dynamics F-16 is the fighter success story of the 1970's and 1980's. It was the winner of the NATO fighter design competition in the early seventies and entered service with the Air Force and several other countries in the mid-seventies. Ultimately, several thousand will be built and flown by the air forces of perhaps 40 countries. The tiny, single-engine jet is just about the most astonishing dogfighter on the scene today, able to accelerate vertically and crank out 9-G turns until the pilot passes out. (This is actually a serious problem with the Falcon, since the plane can easily dish out more Gs than most humans can take.)

The Falcon is also designed to put in duty as a computerized attack bomber, and its capabilities in this area are equally impressive. The majority of Israeli F-16s are two-seaters set up as bombers with a weapons officer in the back seat.

Computerized flight controls are another hallmark of the F-16. All control surfaces, instead of being mechanically linked directly to the control stick, are "fly-by-wire," told what to do by a computer. The computer takes its direction from a small, side-stick controller on a console on the right side of the cockpit. This has earned the F-16 the nickname "Electric Jet." The pilots say it all takes some getting used to, but once they've got it, look out. Other jets may have more impressive long-range weapons systems and radars, but nothing flying can do any better in a close-in knife fight.

A close-up of Arizona Air National Guard Falcon from tanker.

55

The Air Force Flight Demonstration Team, The Thunderbirds, fly F-16 Falcons with only three feet between wingtips.

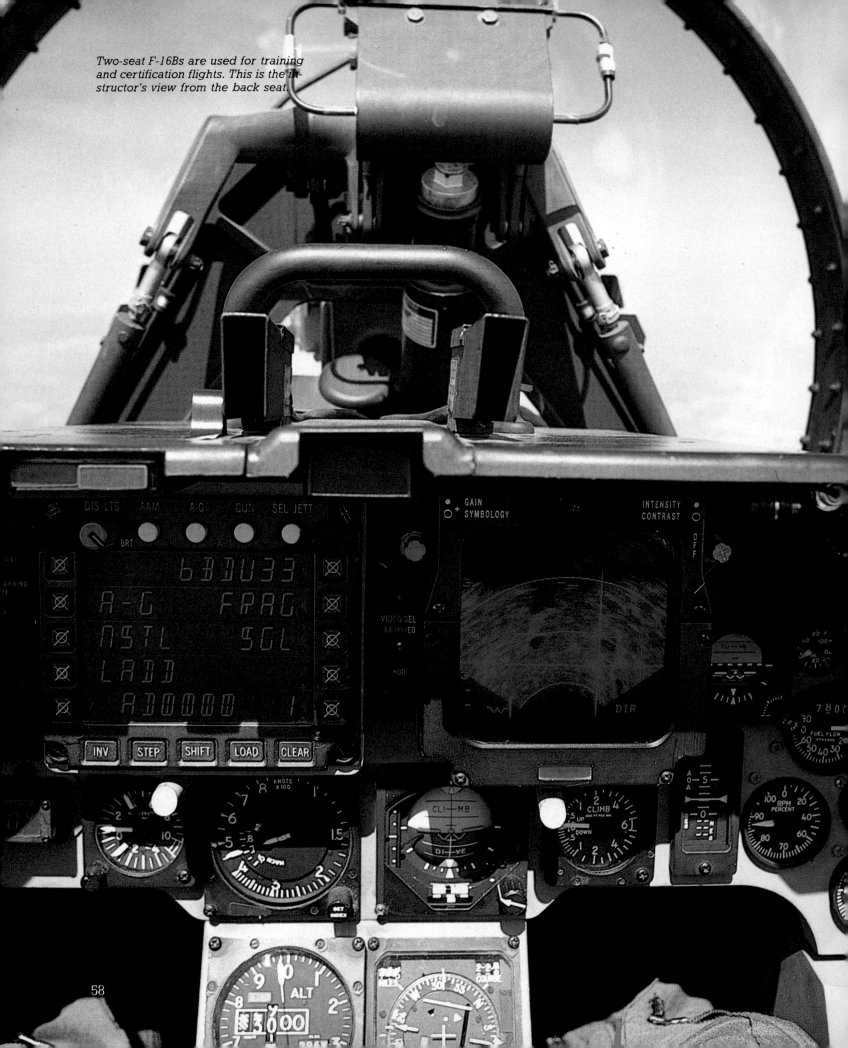

Two-seat F-16Bs are used for training and certification flights. This is the instructor's view from the back seat.

-16s carry video-gun cameras that record every moment of every aerial engagement. Here, the red-hot Falcon pilot is holding the gunsight "pipper" on a hapless F-15.

An instructor relaxes in the back seat while a Montana Air Guard trainee goes through the preflight checklist.

The Falcon pilot's left hand takes care of engine throttle. Under each finger is a control for one or more weapons and radar systems. His right hand is on a side stick controller that replaces the between-the-legs joystick common to all other fighters.

A Falcon driver tightens up his parachute harness before strapping on the "Electric Jet."

HIGH SPEED BOOM

A Falcon pilot's view of a friendly KC-0135 tanker during refueling. Boom atop center is inserted by tanker boom operator into the fuel receptacle behind the cockpit.

60

A menacing head-on view of a Tuc-
son Air Guard Fighting Falcon.

Two Falcons form up beneath the viewing window of their refueling tanker. Each jet is loaded with Side-winder missiles on the wingtips, a pair of extra fuel tanks inboard, and practice bomb racks on the outer stations.

63

A Falcon jock mounts up for a night hop at Hill AFB, Utah.

64

SPECIFICATIONS

F-16 FIGHTING FALCON

Manufacturer: General Dynamics

Military branch: Air Force, Air National Guard, Navy

Type: Multi-role fighter

Engine: One Pratt & Whitney F100-200 afterburning turbofan

Maximum speed: 1,350 mph (Mach 2.05)

Wingspan: [With missiles] 32 ft. 10 in.; [without missiles] 31 ft.

Length: 47 ft. 7¾ in.

Height: 16 ft. 8½ in.

Weight: [Empty] 16, 234 lb.; [maximum loaded] 35,400 lb.

Weapons systems: One 20-millimeter M61A-1 gun; bomb and missile maximum load 20,450 lb.

Crew: Pilot

First flight: 1974

Service entry: 1978

F/A-18 HORNET

Marine Corps F/A-18 Hornet viewed from the open rear ramp of a KC-130 Hercules tanker. Leading-edge wing slats are automatically deployed for slow-speed flight of only 150 knots.

"Two-in-One"

Designed in the early seventies, the McDonnell Douglas-Northrop Hornet is the current darling of Naval and Marine Corps aviation. This mid-size jet is a true, dual-role fighter/bomber, as good at air-to-air dogfighting as it is at attacking ground targets. The Hornet can engage effortlessly in an air-to-air dogfight immediately after climbing off a target run. On the aircraft carriers, it will gradually replace the aging A-7 light-attack jet; it's a bit better than the A-7 as a bomber and worlds better in an air battle.

Like the F-14 and F-15, the Hornet is a two-holer (it has two engines, a pair of General Electric F-404 turbofans cranking out some 40,000 pounds of thrust with the afterburners lit). Like the F-16, all flight controls are computerized and fly-by-wire, although the Hornet has a more conventional full-movement control stick between the pilot's legs. All sorts of necessary information about navigation, weapons readiness, and the whereabouts of the enemy are projected on a trio of television/radar screens and onto a "HUD," or Head-Up Display. The HUD is a clear glass panel, set at an angle in the pilot's line of vision, on which information from the instruments is constantly projected. Thus, the Hornet pilot can fly and fight with very little need to look down into the cockpit.

A Hornet looking for a fight over the Yuma, Arizona, ACM (Air Combat Maneuvering) range.

Marine Hornets over the Sierra Nevada mountains, on their way to a Guard-sponsored dogfighting meet at Klamath Falls, Oregon.

Plane captain helps Marine squadron skipper Lt. Col. Manfred "Fokker" Rietsch into his Hornet.

New Hornets under construction at
McDonnell Douglas, St. Louis.

A carrier crew member preflights a
Navy Hornet prior to catapult launch.

"Star Wars" panel of the F/A-18 projects most important information onto
a trio of cathode-ray screens.

A forward-looking pod camera
catches a Hornet closing on the "six"
of several squadron mates.

A Hornet taxis for a night mission at Marine Corps Air Station, El Toro, California.

SPECIFICATIONS

F/A-18 HORNET

Manufacturer: McDonnell Douglas Aircraft Company; Northrop Corporation

Military branch: Marine Corps, Navy

Type: Carrier- and land-based fighter and attack

Engines: Twin General Electric F404-400 afterburning turbofans

Maximum speed: 1,190 mph (Mach 1.80)

Wingspan: [With missiles] 40 ft. 4¾ in.; [without missiles] 37 ft. 6 in.

Length: 56 ft.

Height: 15 ft. 3½ in.

Weight: [Empty] 23,050 lb.; [maximum loaded] fighter 36,710 lb.; attack 49,224 lb.

Weapons systems: One 20-millimeter M61 gun; nine external weapon stations for missiles, bombs, and rockets, with maximum catapult launch load of 13,400 lb.

Crew: Pilot

First flight: 1978

Service entry: 1982

Four Marine Corps Hornets pose for the camera pod over Wendover, Utah.

F-106
DELTA DART

A Montana Dart executes an exuberant roll for the photographer.

"The Gentleman's Fighter"

The beautiful F-106 was designed in the mid-fifties to serve as an air defense interceptor. The fear in those days was manned enemy bombers, and the Delta Dart was tasked to head off the opponents at high speed and launch radar missiles at their formations.

The F-106 has long been regarded as a "gentleman's fighter," a hot and enormously powerful jet that's a dream to fly. But it's sadly outdated, and any of the modern teen fighters can fly circles around it in a dogfight. It's the only fighter in this book that has never seen a minute of actual combat, and it never will.

Despite all this, the Air Guard is saddened to say goodbye to the F-106. The 30-year-old jets are maintained like rare classic cars, painted in gleaming epoxy and waxed regularly. A sad fate awaits most of the lovely birds: They will be converted to supersonic target drones for practice missile shoots.

A trio of New Jersey Air Guard F-106 Delta Darts enters the landing break at Tyndall AFB, Florida.

Montana Air Guard F-106s, although thirty years old, are maintained in like-new condition by dedicated ground crews, many of whom have worked on these same jets for almost twenty years.

A Montana Air Guard F-106 lights the pipe for a full-power takeoff at Great Falls.

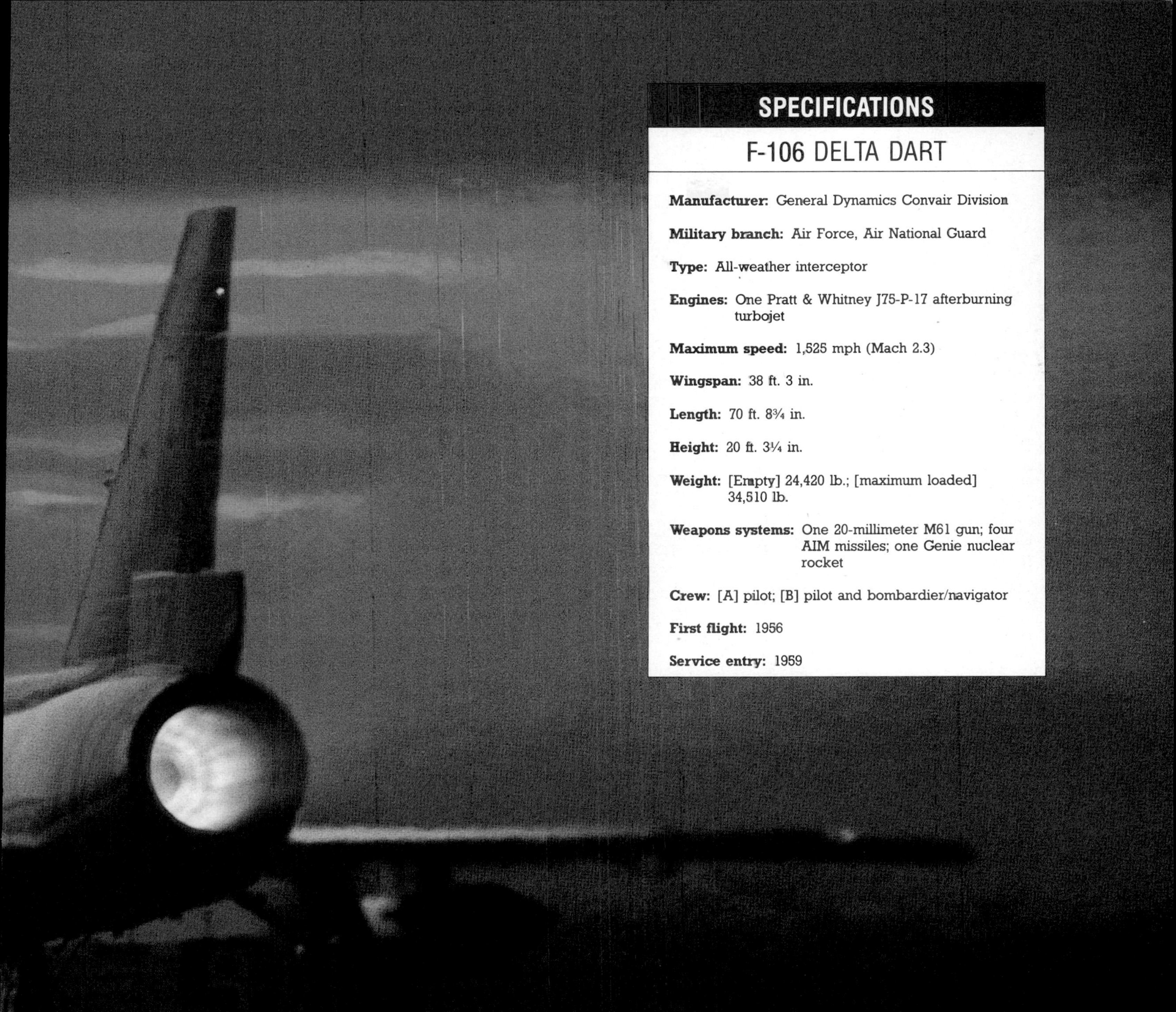

SPECIFICATIONS

F-106 DELTA DART

Manufacturer: General Dynamics Convair Division

Military branch: Air Force, Air National Guard

Type: All-weather interceptor

Engines: One Pratt & Whitney J75-P-17 afterburning turbojet

Maximum speed: 1,525 mph (Mach 2.3)

Wingspan: 38 ft. 3 in.

Length: 70 ft. 8¾ in.

Height: 20 ft. 3¼ in.

Weight: [Empty] 24,420 lb.; [maximum loaded] 34,510 lb.

Weapons systems: One 20-millimeter M61 gun; four AIM missiles; one Genie nuclear rocket

Crew: [A] pilot; [B] pilot and bombardier/navigator

First flight: 1956

Service entry: 1959

F-111
AARDVARK

An F-111 strikes an elegant pose beneath a KC-135 tanker over the North Sea.

"The 'Vark"

The enormous F-111 is more than just a fighter. The Aardvark is an amazingly capable, all-weather penetration bomber, able to strike at extreme ranges and very high speeds, with fifteen tons of deadly ordnance. The Strategic Air Command operates a group of Aardvarks with the FB-111 designation. U.S. Air Force F-111s recently attacked Libya in a complex mission that required the crews to fly 14 hours to and from their bases in England.

The F-111 started life as the all-purpose "TFX" fighter in the early sixties, a dream plane that would be able to do practically every job on land base or carrier. Things didn't work out that way, of course; efforts to make the plane do too much left it overweight, underpowered, and far too complex. The Navy ultimately gave up on the Aardvark, leaving the plane's future to the U.S. Air Force (and the Australians, who bought it). The F-111 is now employed very successfully at bases in Europe and the western U.S. There is also a radar-jamming version, the EF-111 Raven, which accompanies the strike package to the target.

The F-111 can take off at fully loaded weights of approximately 100,000 pounds—far more than the four-engine bombers that flew over Europe in World War II. It is powered by the same TF-30 turbofans that drive the F-14; with its variable-sweep wings cranked back into full sweep, the big 'Vark can break the sound barrier at sea level, a feat few jets can achieve. The plane carries a crew of two, seated side by side: pilot on the left, bombardier/navigator on the right.

*A huge F-111 takes off in full burner
from RAF Lakenheath, England.*

A Lakenheath F-111 tanks over the English Channel. Aardvarks on the 14-hour Libya raid had to refuel eight hair-raising times.

Despite its "F" designation, the F-111 is actually more a penetration bomber than a fighter. It has an internal bomb bay as well as underwing stations that can carry a variety of deadly ordnance.

A two-member Aardvark crew straps in at Lakenheath. The pilot is on the cockpit's left, and the bombardier/navigator sits on the right.

SPECIFICATIONS

F-111 AARDVARK

Manufacturer: General Dynamics Corporation

Military branch: Air Force

Type: Fighter; all-weather attack

Engines: Twin Pratt & Whitney TF30 afterburning turbofans

Maximum speed: 1,450 mph (Mach 2.20)

Wingspan: [Full sweep] 31 ft. 11½ in.; [full spread sweep] 63 ft.

Length: 73 ft. 6 in.

Height: 17 ft. 1½ in.

Weight: [Empty] 46,172 to 53,600 lb.; [maximum loaded] 114,300 to 119,000 lb.

Weapons systems: Weapon bay for two B43 bombs or one B43 and one M61 gun; three pylons under each wing for maximum ordnance load of 31,500 lb.

Crew: Pilot; bombardier/navigator

First flight: 1964

Service entry: 1967

An F-111 peels gracefully away after quick refueling stop over the North Sea.

93

An Air National Guard A-7 Corsair II poses beneath refueling tanker. This is a two-seat "K" model used for training and certification flights.

94

ATTACK JETS

Fighter pilots always seem to get the glory. When Hollywood comes calling, the first thought is to drop Tom Cruise into a fighter plane—specifically, the F-14 Tomcat. Hollywood drives the attack pilots crazy, and with good reason: The job of the fighters is to cover for attack planes, sweeping the skies clean while the attack planes (or "mud-movers") roll in low to hit the enemy with bombs, rockets, and cannon fire. The real damage done to an enemy advancing on the ground, or across the ocean, will be inflicted by those the fighter pilots would nickname the "attack pukes."

Aerial attack has come a long way since World War II.

The smallest jet-powered attack aircraft of today routinely carry more weapons weight (ordnance) aloft than medium and even heavy bombers could lift with their gasoline engines—maybe ten times as much weight! Also, internal bomb bays are now a rarity, except in huge strategic bombers like the B-1 and B-52. Most attack jets carry their deadly payloads on universal pylons ("universal" because the coupling to which the weapons attach are the same for virtually all countries) arrayed under the wings and on the fuselage center line. "Smart" bombs, which are guided either by laser beams or via a tiny television camera in the nose, make it awfully hard to

miss. Computerized bombing systems allow even beginning attack pilots to place "dumb" (unguided) iron bombs smack atop ground targets on their first few tries.

In this section we'll take a closer look at the current American arsenal of aerial ground-pounders: the little A-4 Skyhawk, the carrier-borne A-6 Intruder and A-7 Corsair II, the supremely ugly but bad-to-the-bone A-10 Thunderbolt (that's its official name, but everyone calls it the "Warthog"), and the AV-8 Harrier, a near-supersonic jet that can hover motionless and land vertically. So, slide into the cockpit and get ready to move some mud.

A-4
SKYHAWK

The "Mongoose" variant of the A-4 Skyhawk jet, used as an adversary fighter by Top Gun instructors at NAS Miramar, California. Stripped of excess weight and equipped with a huge Pratt P-8 engine, the Mongoose is a formidable dogfighter even against the much more modern "teen" jets.

"Scooter"

The little "Scooter" goes back some 30 years in American military service, and it's currently being replaced on the front line as the primary light-attack jet for the U.S. Marine Corps. The Skyhawk is a single-engine, one-person attack bomber with a modified delta wing that is so small it doesn't have to be folded on the carrier deck. Many countries around the world still fly the 'Hawk; Israel swears by them, and, in 1982, Argentina was able to do significant damage to a modern British naval force with a nasty combination of Skyhawks and 500-pound iron bombs.

In its declining years the Skyhawk has assumed an interesting job: flying "adversary" for Navy/Marine air combat training. The Navy's Top Gun school uses a sextet of specially modified A-4Fs, each stripped of excess weight and powered by a huge Pratt & Whitney engine. The little attack bird is thus transformed into a formidable fighter, hot and hard to spot. The Top Gun instructors call this version of the A-4 the Mongoose, and they regularly use it to embarrass F-14 and F/A-18 students in their first few dogfight engagements.

The Marine Corps still operates the Skyhawk as a very effective light attack bird, although the vertical-takeoff Harrier will gradually replace it.

97

A formation of Skyhawks heads back to El Toro from the Yuma bombing range. An underwing pod camera caught this shot.

Plane captain twirls upraised right
hand to signal Skyhawk engine start.
The long rod alongside the nose is
the A-4's nonretractable refueling
probe.

An A-4 on a "final" for a sunset landing at the Marines' expeditionary airfield at Twentynine Palms, California.

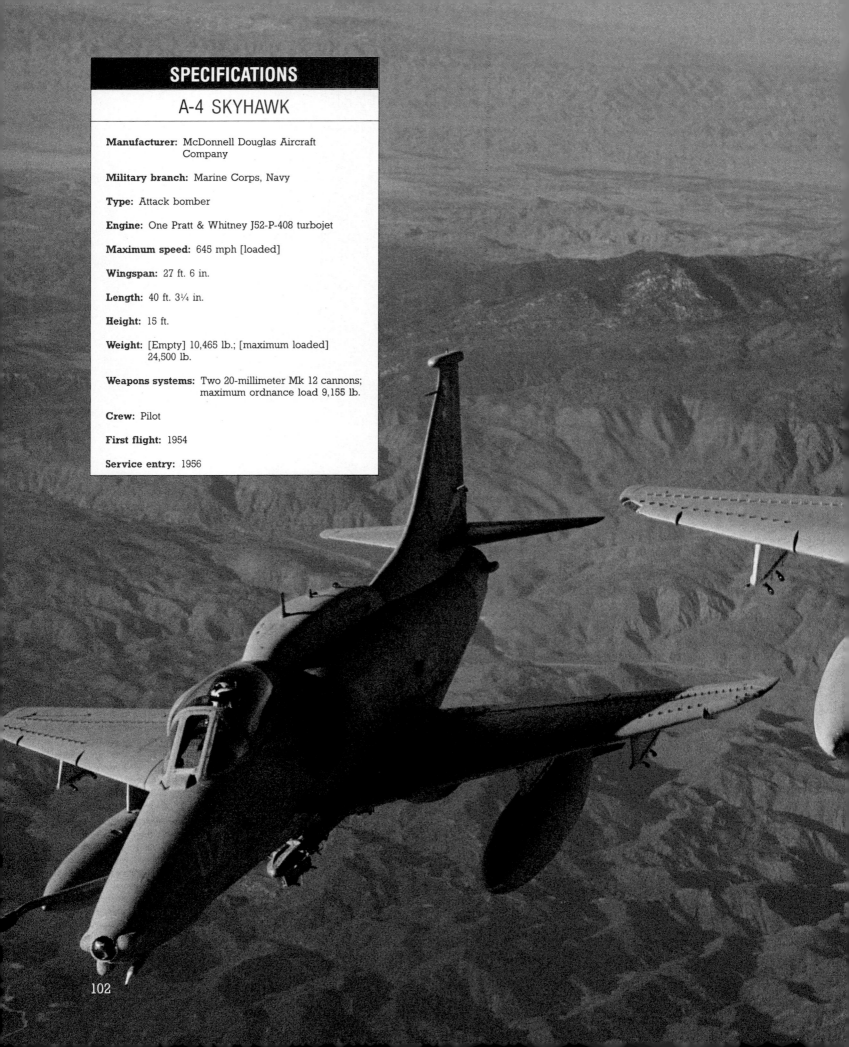

SPECIFICATIONS

A-4 SKYHAWK

Manufacturer: McDonnell Douglas Aircraft Company

Military branch: Marine Corps, Navy

Type: Attack bomber

Engine: One Pratt & Whitney J52-P-408 turbojet

Maximum speed: 645 mph [loaded]

Wingspan: 27 ft. 6 in.

Length: 40 ft. 3¼ in.

Height: 15 ft.

Weight: [Empty] 10,465 lb.; [maximum loaded] 24,500 lb.

Weapons systems: Two 20-millimeter Mk 12 cannons; maximum ordnance load 9,155 lb.

Crew: Pilot

First flight: 1954

Service entry: 1956

A two-ship of Marine A-4s slinging long-range tanks for cross-country hops.

A-6
INTRUDER

A pair of A-6 Intruders sit with wings folded on the deck of the USS Enterprise.

"Heavy Hitter"

There's nothing pretty about the Intruder; in fact, with its bulbous nose and elongated tail it almost looks as if it's flying in the wrong direction. The A-6 is an aircraft carrier's heavy bomber, able to lift off with nine tons of bombs and deliver them night or day, in conditions of absolute zero visibility, with unbelievable accuracy. It's powered by two of the same engines that run the single-engine Skyhawk, and it's flown by a crew of two—a pilot in the left seat, and a navigator-bombardier seated to the right and slightly rearward.

The new A-6F version of the Intruder, due in the fleet by the end of the 1980's, will lead the strike package throughout the 1990's. The F model will be powered by much stronger General Electric F-404 engines—the same as the F/A-18—and the right-seater will have a host of computers, weapons systems, and navigation gear to play with. The strange hooklike device in front of the windshield is the Intruder's aerial refueling probe; by inserting it gently into a hose-and-basket array towed behind an aerial tanker, the big jet can gas up in flight and stay aloft almost indefinitely.

Marine Corps A-6 crew gets ready to go do it. Pilot is on cockpit's left; bombardier/navigator sits to the right and slightly rearward.

Intruders, here mixed with other elements of the carrier air wing, provide the all-weather heavy bombing capability.

Steam pours from the catapult track as an Intruder is "shot" off the waist cat.

An Intruder blurs into motion as
catapult officer signals for a "shot."

Multiple-ejector bomb racks hang beneath the wings of this Intruder as the carrier deck crews chain it to the deck.

The strangely proportioned A-6 is not a beauty contest winner. But then it isn't called upon to perform pretty work. The hooklike device in front of the cockpit is the Intruder's non-retractable refueling probe.

SPECIFICATIONS

A-6 INTRUDER

Manufacturer: Grumman Aerospace Corporation

Military branch: Marine Corps, Navy

Type: Carrier-based all-weather attack

Engines: Two Pratt & Whitney J52-8A turbojets (A, B, C, E); two General Electric F404-400D turbofans (F)

Maximum speed: 684 mph

Wingspan: 53 ft.

Length: 54 ft. 7 in.

Height: 15 ft. 7 in.

Weight: [Empty] 25,630 to 34,581 lb.; [maximum loaded] 60,400 lb.

Weapons systems: Maximum bomb load 15,000 lb.

Crew: Pilot; navigator/bombardier

First flight: 1960

Service entry: 1963

A-7
CORSAIR II

A two-seat Air National Guard A-7K Corsair II slides into refueling position beneath a KC-135 tanker. The open refueling receptacle is visible midwing.

"Honored Name"

The stubby A-7 Corsair II is manufactured by Vought Aircraft, which also made the famed Corsair carrier fighter/bomber of World War II.

The A-7 is a worthy successor to the honored Corsair name. The A-7 evolved from a supersonic fighter of the 1950's, the F-8 Crusader—a plane that can bring tears to the eyes of older Navy jet jockeys; many consider it the most dramatic fighter of all time. The A-7 holds down the light-attack job on most Navy carriers, although it's being replaced one ship at a time by the vastly more capable F/A-18 Hornet. The U.S. Air Force and several foreign air forces also operate A-7s in differing configurations.

The single-engine, single-pilot Corsair has a total of eight weapons stations, six under the wings and two on the body, on which can be hung a deadly array of bombs, rockets, air-to-ground missiles, and electronics pods. It can also sling a pair of Sidewinder heat-seeking missiles on rails under the canopy, in case enemy fighters are loitering as the attack jets come off the bomb point. But the Corsair is a bomber, not a fighter; a lucky quick shot is all the A-7 pilot is ever likely to get off in an aerial engagement.

A Navy A-7 taxis for takeoff on the deck of the USS Kitty Hawk.

Steam huffs from the catapult as an A-7 is positioned for carrier takeoff.

Navy A-7 Corsair rolls in on a practice bomb run over the Fallon, Nevada, range.

The Corsair's huge air intake has a fearful reputation for gobbling FOD (foreign objects that can damage turbine blades) and even, horrifyingly, an occasional deck crew member. The deck of an aircraft carrier is reputed to be the most dangerous place in the world to work.

SPECIFICATIONS

A-7 CORSAIR II

Manufacturer: Vought Systems Division of LTV, Vought Corporation

Military branch: Air Force, Air National Guard, Navy

Type: Carrier-based tactical attack

Engine: One Pratt & Whitney TF30-6 turbofan (A); one Allison TF41-1 turbofan (D, H, K); one Allison TF41-2 turbo fan (E)

Maximum speed: 690 mph

Wingspan: 38 ft. 9 in.

Length: 46 ft. 1½ in.

Height: 16 ft. ¾ in.

Weight: [Empty] 19,781 lb.; [maximum loaded] 42,000 lb.

Weapons systems: Two 20-millimeter Mk12 cannons, six wing, and two fuselage pylons for maximum weapon load of 15,000 lb. (A, B); one 20-millimeter M61 Vulcan gun (D, E) maximum external load of 15,000 lb. of missiles, bombs, rockets, gun pods, fuel tanks

Crew: Pilot

First flight: 1965

Service entry: 1966

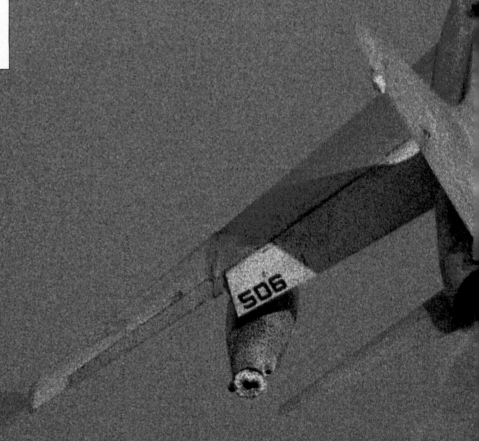

A Corsair banks effortlessly away from the carrier after a good "cat shot."

A-10
THUNDERBOLT II

A-10 Warthogs fly in formation over their base at RAF Bentwaters, England.

"The Warthog"

While the F/A-18 and F-111 are multirole designs, the A-10 Thunderbolt II, universally nicknamed the Warthog, is the opposite. It is an aircraft designed for one specific job only. The oddly proportioned Hog is a close-air-support bird, pure and simple—at its best when it's low, slow, and eyeball to eyeball with the enemy's ground forces.

Although the A-10 is powered by two big turbofans, it's a slow mover, scarcely one third as fast as the teen fighters.

Its huge, straight wing helps it achieve matchless low-speed maneuverability and accuracy as a weapons platform. The Hog is also designed to take hits from ground fire and keep on trucking; the pilot (and ejection seat) is surrounded by an armored "bathtub" and the plane is built with double, triple, and even quadruple-redundant control and fuel systems. The landing gear retracts only halfway, permitting emergency landings with the main wheels protruding.

The A-10 was designed and built around its principal armament, a 30-millimeter antitank gun with seven rotating barrels. The big gun spews out six-inch rounds loaded with spent uranium that can blast through the armor of the heaviest tank. (Spent uranium is nonradioactive and probably the heaviest metal around.) Warthogs are flown by the active Air Force in Europe and Korea, and by the Reserve and National Guard in the U.S.

124

Air Force Reserve "Hog" driver J.D. McCoy is dwarfed by hulking A-10.

125

An A-10 meets up with its mobile gun loader at an austere desert base in Nevada.

A Warthog pulls up sharply after scoring a direct bomb hit.

The immense GAU-8 Avenger cannon is the heart of the A-10; the airplane was actually designed around the seven-barrel gun and its magazine of 1,100 spent-uranium rounds.

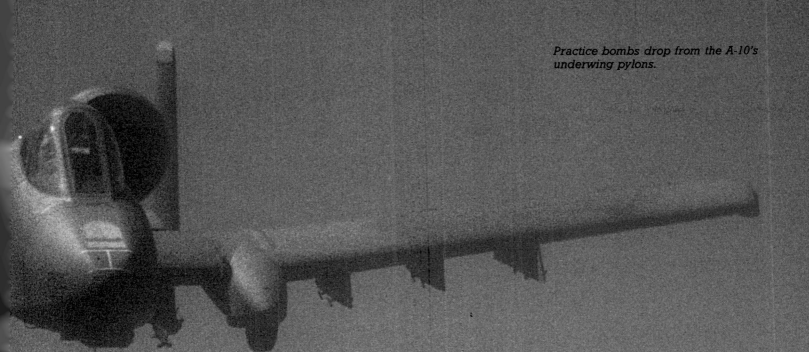

Practice bombs drop from the A-10's underwing pylons.

The A-10's huge seven-barrel cannon fires 30 millimeter spent-uranium rounds. Spent uranium is nonradioactive and extremely heavy, giving the antitank rounds tremendous kinetic energy.

The front office of an A-10. Yellow ejection seat handles are on either side of the seat and various weapons-release buttons stud the center control stick.

Air Force Reserve Warthog out of NAS New Orleans en route to Mississippi bombing range.

130

SPECIFICATIONS

A-10 THUNDERBOLT II

Manufacturer: Fairchild Republic Company

Military branch: Air Force, Air National Guard

Type: Close-support attack

Engines: Twin General Electric TF34-100 turbofans

Maximum speed: 423 mph

Wingspan: 57 ft. 6 in.

Length: 53 ft. 4 in.

Height: 14 ft. 8 in.

Weight: [Empty] 21,519 lb.; [maximum loaded] 50,000 lb.

Weapons systems: One GE GAU-8/A Avenger 30-millimeter gun; external ordnance maximum load 16,000 lb.

Crew: Pilot

First flight: 1972

Service entry: 1975

AV-8B HARRIER

An AV-8A Harrier provides the Marine Corps with front-line attack capability even if conventional airfields are damaged or unavailable.

"The 'Jump' Jet"

Marine attack pilots operate the most unusual jet in the whole American military inventory, the astonishing AV-8B Harrier. The Harrier is a British-designed attack craft that can direct the thrust of its Rolls-Royce engine to take off or land vertically and to hover in flight like a big, noisy hummingbird. This gives the Marines a strong and fast ground-attack plane that can be operated from tiny airstrips near the battlefield or from small flight decks on ships of almost any size.

British and Marine Harrier pilots have also developed a bag of dogfighting tricks that no other fighter can match. By moving the four thrust nozzles while turning the plane, the pilot can tighten the radius of the turn unnaturally—a big advantage when fighting air-to-air. The nozzles can even be cranked forward to slow the little jet in level flight, a great way to force an adversary to overshoot and get in front of the Harrier (and its missiles and 25-millimeter gun). This is called presenting your "six," referring to the clock system of designating the area around the plane—12 o'clock is dead ahead, 6 o'clock is dead behind. A small handful of English Harriers did terrible damage to the much larger Argentine Air Force using these unnerving tactics in the Falklands War of 1982.

*An AV-8 Harrier vectors its thrust
nozzles downward in order to hover
in mid-air.*

Four rotating thrust nozzles, two on each side of the Harrier's fuselage, can be turned from straight, to aft, to straight down for vertical takeoffs and landings.

134

A Harrier drops in vertically with thrust nozzles pointed downward.

SPECIFICATIONS

AV-8 HARRIER

Manufacturer: British Aerospace, McDonnell
Aircraft Company

Military branch: Marine Corps

Type: Carrier- or land-based close-support attack

Engine: One Rolls-Royce Pegasus vectored-thrust
turbofan

Maximum speed: 668 mph

Wingspan: 30 ft. 4 in.

Length: 46 ft. 4 in.

Height: 11 ft. 8 in.

Weight: [Empty] 13,086 lb.; [maximum loaded]
31,000 lb.

Weapons systems: One 25-millimeter GAU-12/U gun;
seven pylons for maximum
external ordnance load of
17,000 lb.

Crew: Pilot

First flight: 1978

Service entry: 1983

The AV-8B Harrier II is a much-improved follow-on aircraft, with a larger engine, more fighting capability, and greater stability in the hover mode.

A Mach 3 SR-71 Blackbird poses beneath a tanker over northern California.

138

RECONNAISSANCE PLANES

Reconnaissance is a tough job. The crew spends long hours in the cockpit over enemy lines with nothing to shoot with but cameras. Recon pilots depend on various combinations of high speed and high altitude to keep out of trouble and out of reach. The tactical reconnaissance crews usually do their stuff down low on the deck at the speed of heat—and that's fast!

The technology for these planes is awesome. The breathtaking SR-71 Blackbird and high-altitude TR-1 and U-2 gather intelligence and scientific data on a strategic, or global, scale. Tactical intelligence gatherers like the specially modified RF-4 Phantom get down in the weeds over the battle area to give top commanders the up-to-date, onsite information they need to win the war. Specifically dedicated (doing only one task) recon birds are on the way out, though. The trend is toward multicapable planes: Camera and data pods can be quickly slung under the wings of fast fighters like the F-14, F-16, and F/A-18 for tactical intelligence gathering.

Reconnaissance is, by its very nature, shrouded in secrecy. One side doesn't want the other side to know just how it gathers intelligence behind enemy lines. But, to find out what we can, let's join our recon jockeys as they fly high and low to scope out the information that has become so strategic to our defense.

139

SR-71
BLACKBIRD

Boom operator lowers refueling probe as SR-71 positions itself for gas-up.

"The Fastest"

The most exotic jet in American military history is the SR-71 Blackbird, a quarter-century-old design that remains the world's fastest military aircraft. The Blackbird's jockey can light the afterburners on its Pratt & Whitney J-58 turbojets and cruise at Mach 3.31—that's three times the speed of sound, or 2,193 miles per hour. The Blackbird spends most of its time in the thin, frigid air of the tropo-sphere, 80,000 feet above the earth, where no interceptor or missile can touch it.

The SR-71 carries no weapons; it is a strategic reconnaissance aircraft, capable of gathering the photographic and electronic intelligence data that eludes the spy satellites in space. The name Blackbird comes from its "paint job," a covering of microscopic iron balls that absorbs radar.

Its crew of two is garbed in full space suits, like those worn by the early astronauts. Only twenty-some Blackbirds were built (we've never really known exactly how many); today they fly daily intelligence missions from their home base at Beale Air Force Base, California, and from forward operating detachments at Royal Air Force Milden-hall, England, and Kadena Air Force Base, Okinawa.

The Blackbird slides into precontact position below its specially equipped KC-135Q tanker. The amazing jet burns special JP-7 jet fuel in its J-57 engines.

A sinister-looking Blackbird taxis into Beale AFB, California, at dusk.

The Blackbird is a huge jet, almost as long as a 727 airliner. Its crew of two sits in tandem; both wear full space suits and helmets.

SPECIFICATIONS

SR-71 BLACKBIRD

Manufacturer: Lockheed-California Company

Military branch: Air Force

Type: All-weather strategic reconnaissance

Engines: Two Pratt & Whitney J58-1 afterburning turbojets

Maximum speed: 2,193 mph (Mach 3.31)

Wingspan: 55 ft. 7 in.

Length: 107 ft. 5 in.

Height: 18 ft. 6 in.

Weight: [Empty] approximately 60,000 lb.; [maximum loaded] 170,000 lb.

Weapons systems: None

Crew: Pilot, systems officer

First flight: 1962

Service entry: 1964

RF-4
PHANTOM

The photo-reconnaissance variant of the venerable Phantom has speed and surprise as its only weapons. Nose-mounted cameras and sensors are the main visible differences.

"Speed and Surprise"

The unarmed, all-weather photo-reconnaissance version of the earlier, venerable F-4 Phantom has one of the toughest missions in modern aerial warfare: It streaks alone over the target before and after the strike, photographing enemy installations and then assessing damage. The motto of the RF-4 pilots is "Alone, unarmed, unafraid." Speed and surprise are the RF-4's only

weapons, and the photo variant of the Phantom (the fastest of the F-4 family) is up to the job, able to make supersonic passes at ultralow levels. By the time the roar of the twin afterburning engines and the sonic shock wave assault the ground observer, the big jet will be long gone.

An ultrasophisticated bird, the RF-4 can be differentiated from other F-4 Phantoms by the

"chin" (located just under the nose) and side camera windows in the elongated nose. High-speed cameras can snap sharp photos downward and to both sides of the jet, despite speeds that reduce everything seen by the human eye to nothing more than a confused blur.

An RF-4 of the Alabama Air National Guard rolls into the sun before dropping down for a low-level, speed-of-heat photo pass.

148

A recon Phantom dances over the building thunderheads in the Gulf of Mexico.

Photo technician removes film cassettes from camera compartment of Marine Corps RF-4B.

151

Alabama Air Guard RF-4C strikes a handsome pose over the Florida coast.

Photo Phantom rolls into the landing break over its Birmingham, Alabama, base.

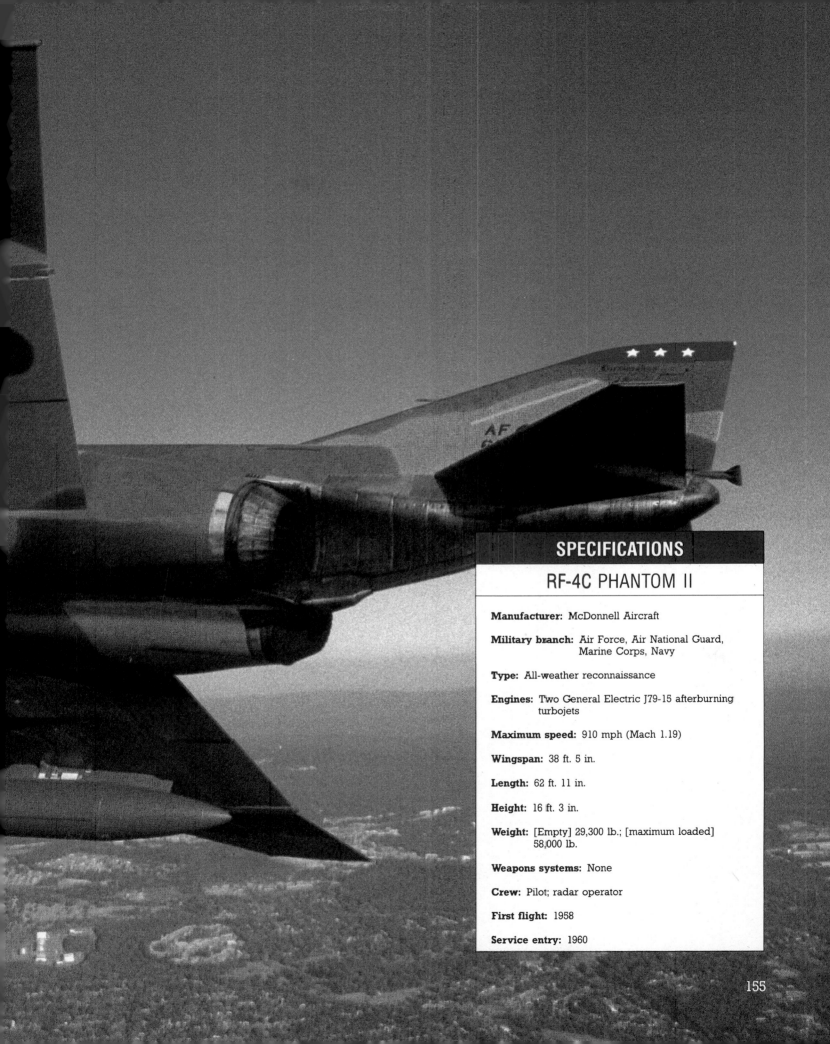

SPECIFICATIONS

RF-4C PHANTOM II

Manufacturer: McDonnell Aircraft

Military branch: Air Force, Air National Guard, Marine Corps, Navy

Type: All-weather reconnaissance

Engines: Two General Electric J79-15 afterburning turbojets

Maximum speed: 910 mph (Mach 1.19)

Wingspan: 38 ft. 5 in.

Length: 62 ft. 11 in.

Height: 16 ft. 3 in.

Weight: [Empty] 29,300 lb.; [maximum loaded] 58,000 lb.

Weapons systems: None

Crew: Pilot; radar operator

First flight: 1958

Service entry: 1960

TR-1

"The Floater"

The gawky Lockheed TR-1 is another strategic recon bird, but it's a slow, quiet floater rather than a streak of lightning like the SR-71 Blackbird. The TR-1 is a modernized (late seventies) version of the famous U-2 spy plane. Both planes have gigantic, thin wings reminiscent of a sailplane or glider; with their small jet engines, they can float for hours on end at tremendously high altitudes. While it has the same basic frame, the TR-1 is much more modern and capable; it has bigger engines and solid-state systems. Its super-sophisticated radar systems can "see" several miles into enemy territory—without ever crossing over enemy borders.

The TR-1's pilot wears a full space suit, like his colleagues in the Blackbird. Sensors and cameras aboard the TR-1 can pull in data from all over the electronic and visible spectrum. In addition, NASA is using the TR-1 for scientific studies related to problems of high-altitude pollution, radioactivity, and the puzzling deterioration of the earth's ozone layer.

The Lockheed TR-1 high-altitude reconnaissance plane is the follow-on version of the famous U-2. It can loiter for hours at ultra-high altitude, gathering photographic and electronic intelligence.

SPECIFICATIONS

TR-1

Manufacturer: Lockheed-California Company

Military branch: Air Force, NASA, Navy

Type: Reconnaissance

Engine: One Pratt & Whitney J75-P-13B turbojet

Maximum speed: 495 mph

Wingspan: 103 ft. 0 in.

Length: 62 ft. 9 in.

Height: 16 ft.

Weight: [Empty] 15,500 lb.; [maximum loaded] 41,300 lb.

Weapons systems: None

Crew: Pilot

First flight: 1981

Service entry: 1981

U-2

Several U-2s have been modified into two-plane trainers, the instructor sitting in the oddly bulging cockpit behind the student.

"Odd Bird"

The U-2 is an odd bird indeed—quite unlike any other jet in this book. Dating from 1955, the U-2 is a single-engine, ultra-high-altitude reconnaissance aircraft. Its long, straight wings are designed to permit the plane to operate as a powered glider, capable of loitering for many hours at altitudes well above 75,000 feet.

Those big wings also permit the U-2 to carry an impressive variety of data-collection instruments and equipment—cameras, infrared sensors, and gadgets for sampling radioactivity and ozone depletion in the upper atmosphere. In fact, Air Force U-2s have increasingly been used for nonmilitary missions—high-altitude study of violent weather patterns leading to tornadoes and hurricanes, the search for geothermal energy sources in the ground, crop estimates and flood-control studies for the Department of Agriculture, even for wide-ranging searches for men and ships lost at sea.

Like the crewmembers in the SR-71, the U-2's pilot wears a full space suit at all times in the cockpit. The aircraft's published top speed is over 400 mph, but the odd bird spends most of its hours at much slower airspeeds. On its lumbering but strangely elegant takeoff run, the jet's drooping wing tips are kept from scraping the concrete by a pair of "training wheels," which fall to the ground as the plane slowly picks up speed. These huge wings make the U-2 a real bear to fly, especially in the low-speed regimes associated with takeoff and landing.

SPECIFICATIONS

U-2

Manufacturer: Lockheed-California Company

Military branch: Air Force

Type: High-altitude strategic reconnaissance

Engines: One Pratt & Whitney J75-P-13B turbojet

Maximum speed: 430 mph

Wingspan: 103 ft.

Length: 63 ft.

Height: 16 ft.

Weight: [Empty] 15,000; [loaded] 41,000 lb.

Weapons systems: None

Crew: Pilot

First flight: 1955

Service entry: 1955

TRAINER JETS

An Air Force advanced jet student about to mount up for a night instrument ride at Vance AFB, Oklahoma.

Future jet pilots in the Air Force, Navy, and Marine Corps make their first flights in relatively simple propeller-driven planes. These birds, forgiving of errors and not burdened with lots of complex systems, allow the sweating student to concentrate on the fundamentals of flight. The instructor in the back seat will call for tougher and trickier maneuvers as dictated by the speed of the student's progress.

At one point, after a practice landing—an electrifying moment in the career of any pilot, one to always be remembered—the instructor will direct the student to the run-up area alongside the runway. The instructor will climb out of the rear cockpit, lean into the front, and shout to the student over the roar of the engine: "Why don't you take it around the pattern by yourself?" In a sense, after the quick solo flight that follows, the thrill is never quite the same.

The students move up into progressively nastier and more unforgiving aircraft as their training progresses, until they're flying advanced trainers that are every bit as hot—in many cases hotter—than the jets they'll fly as combat pilots. If you've ever dreamed of flying jets, here's your chance to see what dues must be paid in order to earn those wings.

T-38
TALON

The beautiful T-38 Talon is the Air Force's advanced jet trainer, capable of dazzling supersonic performance.

"Slippery"

Air Force jet pilots do their advanced work in the beautiful T-38 Talon, a supersonic twin jet with tiny, straight wings and an elongated needle nose. The Talon is a close cousin to the F-5E Tiger II; in fact, the two-seat Tiger and the T-38 are very hard to tell apart.

The T-38 is an ideal advanced trainer because it is fast, slippery, and demanding. Its miniscule wings give it very high wing-loading rates—that is, the number of pounds of airplane per square foot of wing is very high. As a result the Talon takes off and lands at very high speeds, and it glides like a cinder block. But the jet is a joy to fly if the pilot is willing to pay attention and keep ahead of the airplane. A pilot who shines in the Talon will be able to handle any jet in the Air Force, and that's the best thing that can be said about a trainer. The Air Force Flight Demonstration Team, the Thunderbirds, flew T-38 Talons as their show bird for many years before making the transition to the F-16 in the early eighties.

A Talon takes off at Nellis AFB, Nevada. Tiny wings necessitate very high landing and takeoff speeds.

SPECIFICATIONS

T-38 TALON

Manufacturer: Northrop Corporation

Military branch: Air Force, NASA, Navy

Type: Supersonic basic trainer

Engines: Twin General Electric J85-GE-5A afterburning turbojets

Maximum speed: 858 mph (Mach 1.3)

Wingspan: 25 ft. 3 in.

Length: 46 ft. 4½ in.

Height: 12 ft. 10½ in.

Weight: [Empty] 7,164 lb.; [maximum loaded] 11,820 lb.

Weapons systems: None

Crew: Student pilot; trainer

First flight: 1959

Service entry: 1961

Thousands of Air Force pilots have learned the serious stuff in the T-38. It's an ideal trainer—hot, fast, and responsive to the slightest touch. Fly the Talon well, and you can shine in any Air Force fighter.

T-2
BUCKEYE

"Buck"

For future Navy pilots, the first taste of jet flight will come in the T-2 Buckeye, a fat little trainer that will be fondly remembered for its docile and pleasant personality. Budding carrier jockeys will make their first "traps," or arrested landings, in the Buckeye. The instructor will be urging the trainee to slam the plane down onto the steel deck, the jet's arresting hook groping for one of the carrier's four cables strung 10 feet apart. Every carrier landing—indeed every future landing in the carrier pilot's entire career—will be graded by landing-signal officers at the corner of the flight deck. Every pilot is trying for a grade of "OK 3-wire"—a perfect trap where the arresting hook snares the third wire.

Navy fighter pilots will climb back into the "Buck" throughout their careers, for continual training in how to recover from stalls and spins. Even the hottest jets can flop over onto their backs if pushed too far in a dogfight, and the resulting nightmare, known as a "flat inverted spin," is very, very hard to escape. Pilots take the Buckeye up once a year, with a seasoned stall-spin instructor along for the ride, and get seriously upside-down for a couple of gut-wrenching hours. Few pilots consider these training sessions fun. But they'll have a lot less fun

if they ever get into the same kettle of soup with their Phantom or Tomcat.

SPECIFICATIONS
T-2 BUCKEYE

Manufacturer: Rockwell International Corporation

Military branch: Navy

Type: Jet trainer

Engines: Two General Electric J85-GE-4 turbojets

Maximum speed: 530 mph

Wingspan: 38 ft. 1½ in.

Length: 38 ft. 3½ in.

Height: 14 ft. 9½ in.

Weight: [Empty] 8,115 lb.; [maximum loaded] 13,191 lb.

Weapons systems: Gun packs, practice bombs, rockets, and target towing gear; maximum load 640 lb.

Crew: Student pilot; trainer

First flight: 1958

Service entry: 1958

The Navy's basic jet trainer, the docile T-2 Buckeye, is a pleasant and forgiving jet that will introduce the trainee to his first carrier landings and catapult takeoffs.

T-33

"T-Bird"

The ancient "T-Bird" was the Air Force's first jet trainer; it has now been in continuous service for more than forty years. Few of the jets are still operating—maintenance is a nightmarish problem with jets this old—but the Air Force and Air National Guard, as well as some thirty countries around the world, still make limited use of the T-33 as dogfight adversaries and as mock missile targets in air combat maneuvering (ACM) training.

A private aerospace company is trying to sell a modernized version of the T-33 to the many air forces around the world that still operate the plane. The 1980's version is barely recognizable, with its modern pointed nose and its two turbofan engines mounted on the rear fuselage much like the A-10 Warthog. The company has no takers thus far, but there are some 600 T-33s still flying and crying out for modernization.

Manufacturer: Lockheed

Military branch: Air Force, Air National Guard

Type: Trainer

Engine: One Allison J33-A-35 turbojet

Maximum speed: 600 mph

Wingspan: 38 ft. 10½ in.

Length: 37 ft. 9 in.

Height: 11 ft. 8 in.

Weight: [Empty] 8,084 lb.; [maximum loaded] 14,442 lb.

Weapons systems: None

Crew: Student pilot; trainer

First flight: 1948

Service entry: 1960s

The ancient T-33 dates back to the end of World War II. It's still in limited use as a drone target for missile practice.

ELECTRONIC JETS

Military aircraft can no longer be thought of just in terms of fighters and bombers. More-sophisticated and longer-range weapons necessitate advance detection, identification as friend or foe, and warning. Performance of these tasks is as important as the actual fighting.

In the air battle of the future, fighter and attack pilots will face near-impossible tasks if they are deprived of the early detective work performed by the electronics planes. Because early is always better, the advance activity is a must.

Air controllers aboard the E-2 and E-3 AWACS (Airborne Warning And Control System) planes guide the fighters and strike aircraft to the enemy, giving them valuable advance information pulled in by their long-range radar systems. Two amazing jammers, the Navy EA-6B Prowler and the Air Force EF-111 Raven, make life bearable for the attack bombers by confusing enemy missile radars and interrupting enemy radio transmissions. Yet, because of the equipment they carry, these electronic planes are vulnerable to being picked up on the radar screens of the enemy. And, since they perform a very valuable task, the enemy especially wants to knock them out of the sky. It's high-tech vs. high-tech. This is the time that the incredible speed of these planes plays an important part in their missions. A quick turnaround can get them miles away in a matter of moments.

These remarkable intelligence-gathering "spark birds"—technologically sophisticated and very expensive—will spell the difference between success and disaster for the personnel in the field. So, put on your headset and "listen up." The technology will astound you.

The E-2C Hawkeye is the electronic eyes and ears of the carrier battle group.

EA-6B PROWLER

Marine EA-6B Prowler is a stretched version of the A-6 Intruder, with more powerful engines and a second two-member cockpit.

"Radar Buster"

The EA-6B Prowler does its electronic warfare job for Navy aircraft carriers and the Marine Corps. If the Prowler looks a lot like the fat-nosed A-6 Intruder, it's because it's a "stretched" version of the Intruder with an added rear cockpit and larger engines. But unlike its smaller cousin, the Prowler carries no bombs. On its racks are an array of powerful radio and radar transmitters, powered by their own propeller-driven generators, which can be aimed at ground radar stations controlling surface-to-air missiles. With a timely blast of carefully directed radar signals, the ground search radars can be knocked off the air, temporarily or for good. No radars, no SAMs.

Needless to say, the low-level attack guys have a healthy respect for the wizards who work the Prowlers. The big bird is flown by a single pilot; the other three ejection seats are occupied by electronic warfare experts who make life very difficult for the anti-aircraft missile personnel down in the weeds.

Plane captain signals engine start-up for a Navy EA-6B on carrier deck. A conventional A-6 is in the background.

Carrier deck director carefully positions EA-6B on the bow catapult.

173

Marine Prowler lunges into the air at Marine Corps Station Cherry Point, North Carolina. Plane is configured with two fuel tanks and three electronic jamming pods. Small propellers on the pods drive electronic generators that power the radio and radar transmitters.

SPECIFICATIONS
EA-6B PROWLER

Manufacturer: Grumman Aerospace Corporation

Military branch: Marine Corps, Navy

Type: Carrier- and land-based ECM

Engines: Two Pratt & Whitney J52-P-408 turbojets

Maximum speed: 599 mph

Wingspan: 53 ft.

Length: 59 ft. 5 in.

Height: 16 ft. 3 in.

Weight: [Empty] 34,581 lb.; [maximum loaded] 58,500 lb.

Weapons systems: None

Crew: Pilot; three ECM officers

First flight: 1968

Service entry: 1968

The big, heavy EA-6B is a handful for any carrier pilot. Here, a Navy Prowler hooks an "OK 3-wire" on the deck of the USS Enterprise.

177

E-3 SENTRY

"Scope Dopes"

The Air Force player in the AWACS (Airborne Warning And Control System) game is the E-3 Sentry, a militarized Boeing 707 with the antenna stored in the familiar rotating radome on top. (This dome also rotates while in operation.) The capabilities of the AWACS are similar to those of the Hawkeye, only more so; it has far more powerful radars and larger computers. Controllers aboard the AWACS can monitor everything that moves on the ground or in the air as far as 250 miles from the plane.

Because extreme speed is so much a part of modern warfare, the fighters flying toward an impending air battle will rely on the AWACS "scope dopes" (the crew members sitting behind the scopes) to steer them toward an advantageous merge with their opponents, and to give them urgent calls in case other bogies are sneaking up on their six o'clock positions. But since the role of the early warning birds is so important, they are a choice target for enemy attack.

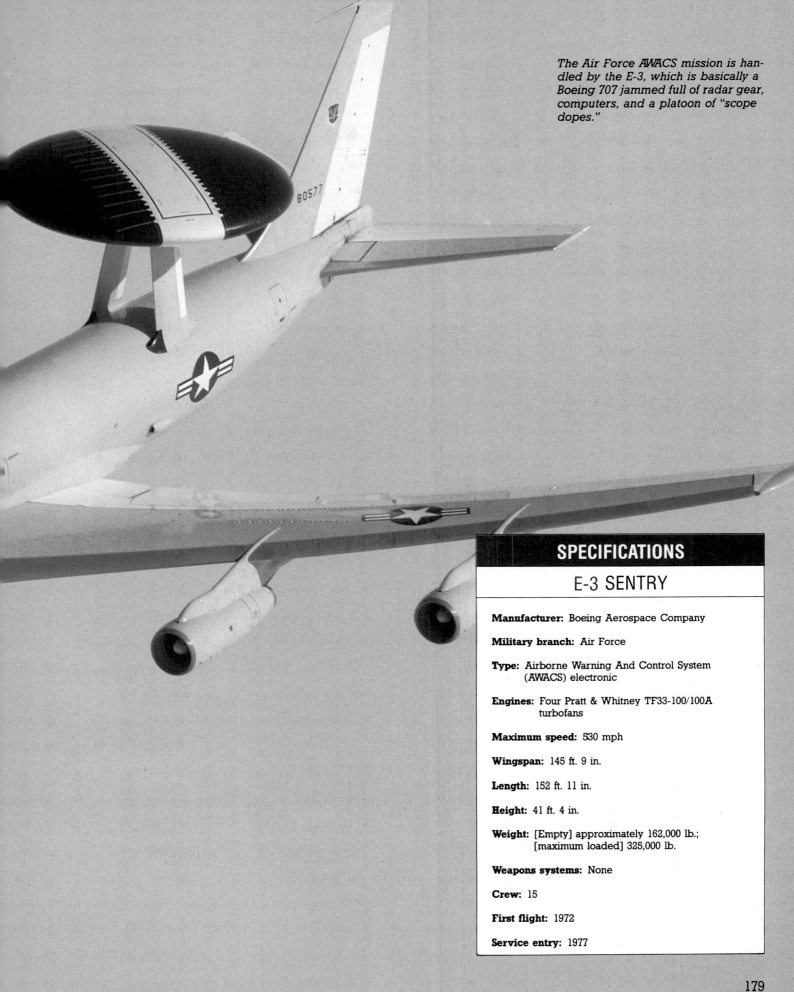

The Air Force AWACS mission is handled by the E-3, which is basically a Boeing 707 jammed full of radar gear, computers, and a platoon of "scope dopes."

SPECIFICATIONS

E-3 SENTRY

Manufacturer: Boeing Aerospace Company

Military branch: Air Force

Type: Airborne Warning And Control System (AWACS) electronic

Engines: Four Pratt & Whitney TF33-100/100A turbofans

Maximum speed: 530 mph

Wingspan: 145 ft. 9 in.

Length: 152 ft. 11 in.

Height: 41 ft. 4 in.

Weight: [Empty] approximately 162,000 lb.; [maximum loaded] 325,000 lb.

Weapons systems: None

Crew: 15

First flight: 1972

Service entry: 1977

E-2C
HAWKEYE

A Hawkeye, its tailhook extended, motors toward the carrier at 125 mph for an arrested landing.

"High-Flying Scanner"

The Hawkeye is the electronic eyes and ears of the carrier Air Wing. That includes fighters, attack jets, helicopters, tankers, antisubmarine patrol craft, and so on. Launched far ahead of the strike and fighter elements, the E-2 loafs at high altitude and orbits in a race-track pattern, scanning three million cubic miles of airspace with its powerful radars. It can monitor friendly and enemy ships, tracking more than 250 tar-

gets at one time. It is even very capable over land. The plane is flown by a crew of two while three controllers in the back monitor scopes and communicate with ships and aircraft by radio and computer data link. The E-2C carries no weapons.

In service since the early seventies, the Hawkeye is a handsome twin turboprop built by Grumman. Its most distinguishing feature is a huge rotating radar

saucer on top; the dish houses its antenna and is actually designed to fly like a wing, thereby compensating for its weight and aerodynamic drag. It can also be lowered for clearance into a hangar. The Hawkeye, despite its large size, is fully carrier-capable, although it has the reputation of being quite a handful to bring aboard the boat.

A group of Hawkeyes, their radomes turning slowly, line up for catapult-assisted takeoffs from their aircraft carrier.

A catapult officer genuflects in the traditional "launch" signal as a Hawk-eye strains at full power on the catapult. In just over two seconds the huge plane will hurtle off the bow at 130 mph.

A Hawkeye loiters at high altitude, flying in a leisurely oval pattern as its radars scan three million cubic miles of airspace.

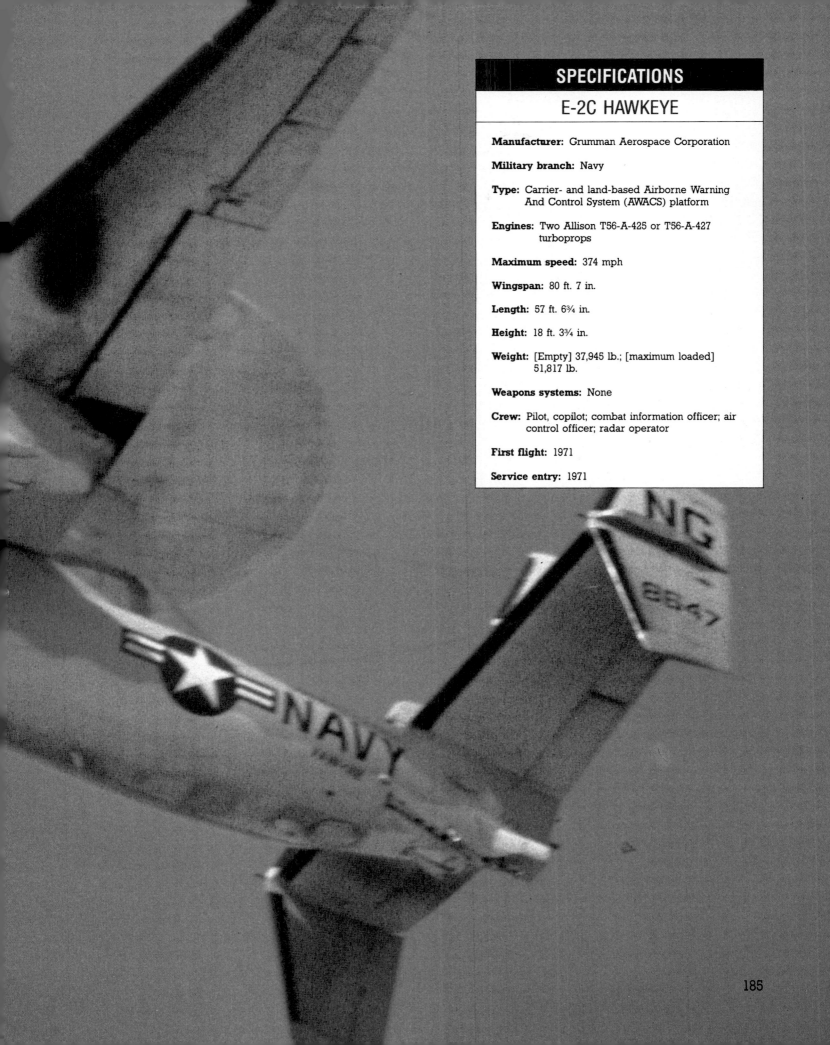

SPECIFICATIONS

E-2C HAWKEYE

Manufacturer: Grumman Aerospace Corporation

Military branch: Navy

Type: Carrier- and land-based Airborne Warning And Control System (AWACS) platform

Engines: Two Allison T56-A-425 or T56-A-427 turboprops

Maximum speed: 374 mph

Wingspan: 80 ft. 7 in.

Length: 57 ft. 6¾ in.

Height: 18 ft. 3¾ in.

Weight: [Empty] 37,945 lb.; [maximum loaded] 51,817 lb.

Weapons systems: None

Crew: Pilot, copilot; combat information officer; air control officer; radar operator

First flight: 1971

Service entry: 1971

F-15 Eagle lights full afterburners
against a Gulf of Mexico sunset.

GLOSSARY

AAA Antiaircraft Artillery. Fired at attacking aircraft from the ground.

ACM Air Combat Maneuvering. Fighter-versus-fighter dogfighting. The Top Gun course is a five-week total-immersion course in ACM.

Afterburner A system that feeds raw fuel into a jet's hot exhaust, thus greatly increasing power output and fuel consumption. A jet in "full burner" will burn almost ten times as much fuel as in normal cruise, so a jet pilot must control the urge to "light the pipes."

AWACS Airborne Warning And Control System. Sophisticated detection aircraft armed with radar and computers.

B/N Bombardier/Navigator. All-important second crew member of the A-6 Intruder and the F-111 Aardvark.

Bandit Dogfight adversary positively identified as a bad guy, either by sight or by a call from a ground or airborne controller.

Bogey Unidentified and potentially hostile aircraft.

CAS Close Air Support. Low-level support of ground troops in combat. CAS is normal work for the attack jets.

Cat shot A carrier takeoff assisted by a steam-powered catapult. A "cold cat," one in which insufficient launch power has been set into the device, can place the hapless aircraft in the water. A "hot cat"—too much pressure—is less perilous, but can rip out the launching bridle or the aircraft's nose wheel assembly. Once a pair of common problems, these are practically unheard of today.

Check six Visual observation of the rear quadrant, from which most air-to-air attacks can be expected. Refers to the clock system of scanning the area around the aircraft: 12 o'clock is straight ahead, 6 o'clock is dead astern. Also a common salutation and greeting among tactical pilots.

Dogfight A term stemming from World War I, referring to the twisting and turning aerial battles between two or more fighter aircraft.

Downtown Where the bad guys hang out. Referred specifically to Hanoi during the Vietnam War.

ECM Electronic Countermeasure. System for jamming or misleading enemy weapons, communications, or radar.

Ejection seat Most of the aircraft in this book are equipped with ejection seats for each crew member. In a critical situation, a powerful rocket motor will blast the pilot and seat out of the aircraft; the parachute automatically opens only three seconds later.

Electric Jet The F-16 Fighting Falcon, so nicknamed because of its fly-by-wire controls.

Fly-by-wire Electronic, computer-controlled operation of aircraft control surfaces. Supplants mechanical/hydraulic actuation common in earlier jets. The F-16 and F/A-18 use these control systems.

FOD Foreign Object Damage. A constant concern on airfields where jets operate. Jet intakes can gulp up loose objects, even as small as a coin or bolt, that can seriously damage delicate turbine blades.

Furball A confused aerial dogfight with many combatants.

G, G-loading, G-rating High-performance jets subject their airframes and occupants to centrifugal force far beyond simple gravity. One G equals normal gravity; a pilot and plane "pulling 4 Gs" in a turn will feel centrifugal force equal to four times the weight of gravity.

G-suit Nylon trousers that wrap around the legs and abdomen. Filled automatically with compressed air in high-G maneuvers, the G-suit helps prevent the pooling of blood in the lower body, thus retarding the tendency to lose consciousness.

Gomer Slang for a dogfight adversary; the usage probably stems from the old *Gomer Pyle* television show.

Ground-pounder Low-level attack aircraft such as the A-6, A-7, and A-10. See *Mud-mover.*

HUD Head-Up Display. A transparent screen mounted on the cockpit dashboard, on which pertinent data from flight instruments and weapons systems are projected. The HUD eliminates the need to look down into the cockpit to read instruments, leaving the pilot free to eyeball the sky in a fight.

Jockey, jock, driver Pilot.

Knife fight Close-in, low-speed aerial dogfight.

Loud handle Lever or grip that fires the ejection seat.

Loud pedal "Stepping on the loud pedal" is slang for pushing the engine throttles full forward to engage the afterburners.

Mud-mover Low-level attack aircraft such as the A-6, A-7, and A-10. The F/A-18 doubles as both fighter and mud-mover. See *Ground-pounder.*

NFWS The Navy Fighter Weapons School. Graduate school for Navy fighter pilots at NAS Miramar, San Diego, California. Its universal nickname is Top Gun, a name borrowed from an old aerial gunnery competition of the 50's.

Nugget Newly minted pilot.

Nylon letdown Ejection.

Pit The rear-seat position of the F-14 Tomcat or the F-4 Phantom.

Radome Streamlined fiberglass enclosure covering a radar antenna, either on the pointed nose of a jet or on a pylon above an AWACS plane like the E-2 and E-3.

RAG Replacement Air Group. Squadron in which newly trained Navy and Marine pilots are introduced and trained in a particular type of aircraft.

Red Flag A large mock air war, held quarterly by the Air Force at Nellis AFB, Las Vegas, Nevada.

Rhino Nickname for the unlovely F-4 Phantom. Also called "Double Ugly."

RIO Radar Intercept Officer. The weapons and navigation expert in the rear seat of the F-14 Tomcat and the F-4 Phantom. See *WIZZO.*

SAM Surface-to-Air Missile.

Scooter Nickname for the A-4 Skyhawk.

Speed of heat Very, very fast.

Speed of thought Even faster than the speed of heat. Also referred to as "Warp One."

TACTS Tactical Aircrew Combat Training System. A system of computers, sensors, data pods, and graphic displays that generates a computer simulation of an actual dogfight for later debrief. In the Air Force, the system is called ACMI, for Air Combat Maneuvering Instrumentation.

Trap Arrested aircraft carrier landing.

Turbofan Jet engine with a large propellerlike fan that impels air into the engine's compressor. The fan also provides propulsion by blowing air around the outside of the compressor. The F-14 and A-10 are turbofan-powered.

Turbojet Older-technology jet engine with a smaller fan that directs air solely through the compressor, where it is mixed with fuel, burned, and exhausted out the tail pipe for rocketlike propulsion. The F-4 and A-7 are turbojet-powered.

Turboprop An engine in which a jet turbine turns an external propeller on a shaft. The E-2 Hawkeye is a turboprop.

Turkey Nickname for the F-14 Tomcat.

Two-holer Jet aircraft with two engines.

VSTOL Vertical or Short Takeoff and Landing. The AV-8 Harrier is a VSTOL aircraft, capable of directing its jet thrust through rotating nozzles to shorten its takeoff roll or to rise and descend vertically.

Warthog Universal nickname for the A-10; no one calls it by its proper name, Thunderbolt II.

Wingman Second pilot in a pair of ships, responsible for ensuring that the leader's six o'clock remains clear.

WIZZO Air Force back-seaters. Stems from Weapons System Officer. See *RIO.*

Air Force Reserve F-16 Falcons catch the last of the sun above the Wendover, Utah, dogfighting ranges.

F-16 Fighting Falcon, the "Electric Jet."

192